P9-EEH-945

REQUIEM FOR A WOMAN
And Selected Lyric Poems

Requiem for a Woman

And Selected Lyric Poems

Rainer Maria Rilke

Translated by Andy Gaus

Introduction by A.S. Wensinger

THRESHOLD BOOKS

Grateful acknowledgment is made to the Wesleyan University *Cardinal* and the *Adlit* of Alpha Delta Phi, where some of these translations first appeared.

Book design by Edmund Helminski

Translations Copyright © 1981 by Andy Gaus

Photograph of Paula Modersohn-Becker - Worpswede Archives

Library of Congress Catalogue Card Number: 80-65910

ISBN 0-939660-00-8

THRESHOLD BOOKS
RD 3, *208, Putney, Vermont 05346

CONTENTS

INTRODUCTION

ONE DAY perhaps fifteen years ago Robert Lowell was being entertained by another celebrated poet and his wife at cocktails and dinner. Lowell had partaken more of the former than the latter, and later in the evening commenced the serio-comic game of naming the Truly Great, a game which I was given to understand had been played not infrequently before. Rilke had already won his medal for German Poets, 20th century, and was well on his way to being crowned by Lowell as the greatest of all poets of our age. The Eliot, Yeats, and Valéry backers would have little of that. I, who had long loved Rilke, did not know the work of the other contenders nearly so well, and was beginning to relish the earnest silliness of it all, was tempted to join Lowell in his corner — despite the fact that I had never been quite won over to his own "Imitations" of Rilke. Still, I felt he was right.

I think I said something like, if we can discount, with a few exceptions, that vast amount of gorgeous, seductive, sentimental, pop-eyed, magnificent stuff Rilke churned out up to about 1900, then there is no other possible choice for the crown. Lowell agreed to the condition; but before any coronation, he had launched into a speech about how the great author of the *Buch der Bilder*, the *Neue Gedichte*, the *Sonetten an Orpheus*, the *Duineser Elegien*, and the late poems had first found his true voice in Paris just after the turn of the century, as secretary to Rodin, and how the great sculptor had been the one to teach him to see and then to say, to reach what Rilke called the *Welt-innenraum*, and to speak with greater objectivity of *die Dinge*, the things of this world.

All this has long been said about Rilke, as Lowell perfectly well knew. And he knew it was an easy and impressive cliche, and that it is true, as far as it goes. But Rodin and Paris did not alone make the new Rilke; nor is any serious critic likely still to say so. Rather, they helped him greatly in his process of refinement and in getting rid of his sometimes insufferable self-centeredness, in making better use of his staggering ego and his even more staggering genius.

There were others involved in this as well, of course, principally his wife Clara Westhoff, the sculptress, and possibly even more important, the painter Paula Modersohn-Becker. It is of the life and death of the latter, a great artist and human being, that Rilke writes in the *Requiem für eine Freundin,* one of his supreme poems.

The major accomplishment of this book is the splendid translation of this long poem by Mr. Gaus. Just as he has given us in brief span a few fine examples from the huge repertoire (still open to those who would join him in putting Rilke into English) through his translations of the shorter poems in this collection — and in very able renditions, indeed — he has not only opened up to English-speaking readers of Rilke some of the poetic amazements of the memorial requiem but has also made available through his complete translation of the work material essential to the study and understanding of an important twentieth-century artist. The poem itself is not easy. A brief word about its background might be worthwhile, for it is a quite extraordinary document of its age, and the principals involved in this background are as intriguing as they are unknown in this country.

Only the slightest sketch can be given in the remainder of this brief introduction. Material abounds for the more curious, nearly all of it in German. Perhaps some day someone will translate the book by H.W. Petzet, *Das Bildnis des Dichters* (1957, second edition 1975), a perceptive if somewhat breathless account of the relationship between Rilke and Modersohn-Becker. It is really a double monograph on the background to the *Requiem* and to Paula's haunting little oil portrait of the poet which hangs in Bremen. As Petzet makes clear to those who might want a summary of this somewhat oracular but fascinating study, Rilke's great poem is not a work which bestows immortality on some minor lady-friend of his, a gifted Sunday painter. Rather it is a work which gives homage, and cries out in sometimes unbearable lamentation, to an artist whom he had finally acknowledged as his equal, to a woman who taught and gave perhaps more to him than he to her. The *Requiem* is one of the great tributes by an artist to an artist in modern literature. Indeed, one might have a hard time in finding its peer. And to be set alongside the poem is Paula's little portrait of the singing poet. Petzet's title means, of course, the portrait of the poet.

At the beginning of their friendship in 1900, however, it was not at all clear to Rilke, or for that matter to any of her friends and acquaintances, that in Paula they were dealing with an important painter. Yet anyone today who might wish to play the artist version of the game of the Truly Great, would have less trouble winning with Modersohn-Becker as candidate in her category than Lowell did with Rilke. For it is by this time fairly generally acknowledged that she is the most important woman artist in the history of modern German art and one of the key figures between Impressionism and Expressionism, male or female, in European art in general.

She was born in 1876 (one year after Rilke) into a large, benevolent, and protective middle-class family in Bremen in Northern Germany. From her letters and journals we get to know a determined, emotional, often frustrated, but also high-spirited and loving person, years ahead of her time in many respects, and also very much the victim of it. Against odds, but also frequently with the fervent backing of her family, she set her sights both on an independent life in Paris and at the same time, tragically, on a domestic and creative tranquility in the small artist colony of Worpswede near Bremen with her husband, the painter Otto Modersohn, twelve years her senior.

During her frequent sojourns in Paris she not only gets to know and see what is afoot in the world of art, discovers for herself Cézanne, Van Gogh, Gauguin, and then Matisse, Nolde, and perhaps even the young Picasso; searches out everything in the Louvre, the Luxembourg, and the other museums and galleries; absorbs the ancients, the Japanese, the Egyptian and Roman painters — but she also, toward the end of her very short life, begins to produce a whole spectrum of canvases herself, especially portraits and self-portraits, in a palette and with experimental techniques which were altogether new in German

9

painting. So new were they, and so disquieting and unexpected at home, that each time upon her return, her acceptance back into the fold, though one of love for her as a person, was almost never one of acclaim for her as an artist. Nevertheless she always did come back. At the end she managed to save her marriage at the brink of disaster, but she lost her life after the birth of her only child. This was in 1907 and she was thirty-one. Like all lives, hers was both utterly simple and utterly complex; its story is essentially one of dignity, honesty, even nobility.

Rilke's role in the story is important, although probably not central. Just what his reaction to her was when they first met in 1900 is hard to say exactly; it is likewise hard to determine the exact degree of their intimacy. It is all but certain, however, that it was not physical; or if by some chance it was for a brief moment, then this aspect of it was swiftly abandoned. Yet Rilke's marriage to Clara seems very much the result of a rebound from Paula. It is perhaps a case of two whose spiritual intimacy was so intense—and in later years, after a severe estrangement, whose artistic aspirations were so keenly attuned— that any physical dimension was really beside the point. In any event, Paula Becker made it clear that her attachment was to Otto Modersohn; and it is significant that throughout their correspondence she and Rilke always address each other with the formal "Sie." The sometimes naive simplicity of Paula's letters stands in sharp contrast to the perfection and felicity of his to her, as indeed the entire corpus of his letters is one of a supreme poetic intelligence and beauty. And yet, Paula seems to have been the more powerful teacher of the two. Rilke says as much in the great poem.

Her power was not clear from the start, and Rilke's realization of it was a long time coming. He first arrived in Worpswede on a commission to write a series of essays in book form on the artists of the colony there. Never once in the entire work does he so much as mention her name, the name of the finest artist of the group. It is strange. Later, when he writes Rodin in Paris, introducing her to the great sculptor, he refers to her merely as "femme d'un peintre allemand très distingué." By this time she had become Modersohn's wife, but also very much a painter in her own right.

At the beginning she had been swept up by the mystic aura and the sensuous and highly charged poetry which Rilke brought with him to the North German moor country from his recent trip with Lou Andreas-Salomé to Russia, where they had, if only briefly, met with Tolstoy. Paula's journal speaks of her very first impressions of him, "a fine and lyrical talent, tender, sensitive, with small and touching hands. He read to us from his poems, gentle and full of presentiment. Sweet and pale." Their times together in her studio seem now almost like set-pieces from fin-de-siècle drama: the "atelier of the lilies," the candlelight, the autumn flowers, his reading aloud from the early angel poems; it is like late pre-Raphaelitism with Jugendstil trappings in a North-German farmhouse studio. Even the style of Paula's writing at the time is strongly affected and she attempts imitations which would be embarrassing now, if it were not that the leaven of her humor and good-hearted and forthright warmth put things back in the proper perspective. Through it all is the aggressiveness of her devotion to Otto. It is an odd set of circumstances.

After this initial period Paula and Rilke were often together in Berlin where he had fled, for whatever reasons. She came out of simple obligation to attend a cooking school in preparation for her marriage. It seems that during this period, and later after the marriage, Rilke wanted both to support her artistic aspirations and construe her as somehow a victim of her family and husband. It is the greatness of her person and ultimately the keystone of their friendship that she refused to play such a role for him. She was a creator, just as much as he was. She was not his raw material. This he finally realized and honored later in Paris, during Paula's several stays there and when they were again often together. He knew her finally as the committed artist she was.

In contrast to all the other women in his life, as Petzet points out, Rilke got to know in Paula Modersohn-Becker probably the only truly creative, not "reproductive," artist. This statement is probably meant to include even Clara herself. He continued to the end to try to "save" Paula from her other self, from her strong domestic and maternal inclinations. He only partly succeeded. She did learn from him or together with him the powerful truth that real love of another consists in letting that person go, in letting him, letting her be alone, be free. The poem speaks wonderfully of this. In turn, he learned from her probably more than from Rodin how to look at things, to see and enter them. Or perhaps they learned that together, too; it is hard to say. In either case, he admits the lesson; and it is a rare confession.

Soon, however, he was obliged to learn of her final acceptance of her other role, of her humility and her return to her husband — and then soon after that of her sudden death. He was dumbfounded, and his reaction was silence. It was not until almost a year later that he composed the *Requiem* in Paris. In three days, from All Hallows Even to All Souls, October 31 through November 2, 1908, he had it complete.

The work can be seen as one great attempt at exorcism. She is the only dead person in his life who weighs upon him. She will not die, although she is dead. She is like his Eurydice and can neither come back nor go away. And the poet expands and by bringing the Paula he knew back for the duration of the poem, he hopes that finally she will leave and lay herself to rest. It is an extraordinary plea. But in one sense it is unlikely that it worked for Rilke, despite its power. For the more one gets to know the story of these two and the better one learns to read Rilke's work from the nearly two decades he outlived Paula, the more it seems she continued to live in him, influencing the creation of much more than just this one work, clinging to him in memory. Clinging or lifting? Dead or transfigured? We may learn to know what the poem says, what those four final lines mean; but we can never know in what ways she remained with him until his own death.

—A.S. Wensinger
Wesleyan University
Middletown. Connecticut

REQUIEM FOR A WOMAN

REQUIEM FÜR EINE FREUNDIN

Ich habe Tote, und ich ließ sie hin
und war erstaunt, sie so getrost zu sehn,
so rasch zuhaus im Totsein, so gerecht,
so anders als ihr Ruf. Nur du, du kehrst
zurück; du streifst mich, du gehst um, du willst
an etwas stoßen, daß es klingt von dir
und dich verrät. O nimm mir nicht, was ich
langsam erlern. Ich habe recht; du irrst
wenn du gerührt zu irgend einem Ding
ein Heimweh hast. Wir wandeln dieses um;
es ist nicht hier, wir spiegeln es herein
aus unserm Sein, sobald wir es erkennen.
   Ich glaubte dich viel weiter. Mich verwirrts,
daß *du* gerade irrst und kommst, die mehr
verwandelt hat als irgend eine Frau.
Daß wir erschraken, da du starbst, nein, daß
dein starker Tod uns dunkel unterbrach,
das Bisdahin abreißend vom Seither:
das geht uns an; das einzuordnen wird
die Arbeit sein, die wir mit allem tun.
Doch daß du selbst erschrakst und auch noch jetzt
den Schrecken hast, wo Schrecken nicht mehr gilt;
daß du von deiner Ewigkeit ein Stück
verlierst und hier hereintrittst, Freundin, hier,
wo alles noch nicht *ist;* daß du zerstreut,
zum ersten Mal im All zerstreut und halb,
den Aufgang der unendlichen Naturen
nicht so ergriffst wie hier ein jedes Ding;
daß aus dem Kreislauf, der dich schon empfing,
die stumme Schwerkraft irgend einer Unruh
dich niederzieht zur abgezählten Zeit —:

I have my dead ones, and. I let them go
And was amazed to see them so consoled,
So soon at home in being dead, so just,
Unlike their reputation. Only you
Return; you graze me, walking round, about
To bump something and make a sound of you,
Betraying you. Oh do not take from me
What I have learned so slowly. You are wrong
If anything at all can move you so
To homesickness. For we transform these things:
They are not here, but mirrored in to us
From out our being, as we catch sight of them.

   I thought you were much farther. It confuses me
That of all people, *you* should wander back,
Who transformed more than any other woman.
That we were frightened when you died, no, that
Your powerful dying darkly interrupted us,
Cutting the Formerly off from the Henceforth,
Is our concern, and to encompass that
Will be the work that we must do with everything.
But that you were afeared and even now
Harbor the fear, where fear is meaningless;
That you should lose a piece of your eternity;
That you should enter here again, friend, here,
Where nothing yet quite *is;* that you, confused,
In your first everything, confused and halfway,
Faced with the opening of the endlesss natures
Could fail to grasp them as you would grasp anything;
That from the circulation that received you,
The wordless sinker of some great unrest
Should pull you down again to counted time —

dies weckt mich nachts oft wie ein Dieb, der einbricht.
Und dürft ich sagen, daß du nur geruhst,
daß du aus Großmut kommst, aus Überfülle,
weil du so sicher bist, so in dir selbst,
daß du herumgehst wie ein Kind, nicht bange
vor Örtern, wo man einem etwas tut —:
doch nein: du bittest. Dieses geht mir so
bis ins Gebein und querrt wie eine Säge.
Ein Vorwurf, den du trügest als Gespenst,
nachtrügest mir, wenn ich mich nachts zurückzieh
in meine Lunge, in die Eingeweide,
in meines Herzens letzte ärmste Kammer,
ein solcher Vorwurf wäre nicht so grausam,
wie dieses Bitten ist. Was bittest du?

Sag, soll ich reisen? Hast du irgendwo
ein Ding zurückgelassen, das sich quält
und das dir nachwill? Soll ich in ein Land,
das du nicht sahst, obwohl es dir verwandt
war wie die andre Hälfte deiner Sinne?

Ich will auf seinen Flüssen fahren, will
an Land gehn und nach alten Sitten fragen,
will mit den Frauen in den Türen sprechen
und zusehn, wenn sie ihre Kinder rufen.
Ich will mir merken, wie sie dort die Landschaft
umnehmen draußen bei der alten Arbeit
der Wiesen und der Felder; will begehren,
vor ihren König hingeführt zu sein,
und will die Priester durch Bestechung reizen,
daß sie mich legen vor das stärkste Standbild
und fortgehn und die Tempeltore schließen.
Dann aber will ich, wenn ich vieles weiß,

16

That wakes me like a burglar in the night.
If I could say you only deign to come
Out of the greatness of your heart's abundance,
Because you are so certain of yourself
That you walk round, a child not yet afraid
Of places where they'll do something to you —
But no: you plead. That is what chills my bones,
Pulling at them like sawteeth back and forth.
A grim reproach brought to me by your ghost,
Brought home to me at night, when I draw back
Into my lungs and into my intestines,
Into the last poor chamber of my heart,
Such a reproach would not be as macabre
As this, your pleading. What are you pleading for?

   Speak: should I travel? Is there anywhere
A thing you left behind that is tormented
And straining after you? Should I explore
A land you never saw, although it was
As close as your brain's other half to you?

   Then I will navigate its rivers, I
Will go on land and ask of ancient customs,
And I will speak with women in the doorways,
Observing how they call their children to them.
I'll notice how they take the landscape in
Around them as they go to the old work
Of fields and meadows; will desire that I
Be led into the presence of the king
And will pay off the priests sufficiently
To set me down before the strongest icon
And go away and close the temple doors.
And finally, when I know these many things,

einfach die Tiere anschaun, daß ein Etwas
von ihrer Wendung mir in die Gelenke
herübergleitet; will ein kurzes Dasein
in ihren Augen haben, die mich halten
und langsam lassen, ruhig, ohne Urteil.
Ich will mir von den Gärtnern viele Blumen
hersagen lassen, daß ich in den Scherben
der schönen Eigennamen einen Rest
herüberbringe von den hundert Düften.
Und Früchte will ich kaufen, Früchte, drin
das Land noch einmal ist, bis an den Himmel.

Denn Das verstandest du: die vollen Früchte.
Die legtest du auf Schalen vor dich hin
und wogst mit Farben ihre Schwere auf.
Und so wie Früchte sahst du auch die Fraun
und sahst die Kinder so, von innen her
getrieben in die Formen ihres Daseins.
Und sahst dich selbst zuletzt wie eine Frucht,
nahmst dich heraus aus deinen Kleidern, trugst
dich vor den Spiegel, ließest dich hinein
bis auf dein Schauen; das blieb groß davor
und sagte nicht: das bin ich; nein: dies ist.
So ohne Neugier war zuletzt dein Schaun
und so besitzlos, von so wahrer Armut,
daß es dich selbst nicht mehr begehrte: heilig.

So will ich dich behalten, wie du dich
hinstelltest in den Spiegel, tief hinein
und fort von allem. Warum kommst du anders?
Was widerrufst du dich? Was willst du mir
einreden, daß in jenen Bernsteinkugeln
um deinen Hals noch etwas Schwere war

Then I will simply watch the animals,
That something of their movements may transpire
Into my joints; will have a short existence
There in their eyes, that hold me and then slowly
Let go, peaceably, without prejudice.
I then will cause the gardeners to recite
Long lists of flowers, so that in the shards
Of their fine Christian names I may bring back
Some trace of all their hundred fragrances.
And I will buy its fruits, its fruits that have
The land inside, as far up as the sky.

 For that was your department: ripened fruits.
You used to put them in the pans before you
And weigh them out upon a scale of colors.
And as you saw the fruits, so you saw women,
And saw the children so, from inside out
Driven into the forms of their existence.
Finally you came to see yourself as fruit;
You peeled yourself of clothes and set yourself
Before the mirror, eased yourself on in,
All but your looking, which remained outside
And did not say *I am* but said *This is.*
So void of curiosity was your looking,
So stripped of gain, of such true poverty,
It no longer desired you even: holy.

 I'd like to keep you where you used to put
Yourself: deep in the mirror, far away
From everything. Why do you come so differently?
Why do you contradict yourself? Why do
You try to make me think that in those beads
Of amber round your neck there was still gravity,

von jener Schwere, wie sie nie im Jenseits
beruhigter Bilder ist; was zeigst du mir
in deiner Haltung eine böse Ahnung;
was heißt dich die Konturen deines Leibes
auslegen wie die Linien einer Hand,
daß ich sie nicht mehr sehn kann ohne Schicksal?
    Komm her ins Kerzenlicht. Ich bin nicht bang,
die Toten anzuschauen. Wenn sie kommen,
so haben sie ein Recht, in unserm Blick
sich aufzuhalten, wie die andern Dinge.
    Komm her; wir wollen eine Weile still sein.
Sieh diese Rose an auf meinem Schreibtisch;
ist nicht das Licht um sie genau so zaghaft
wie über dir: sie dürfte auch nicht hier sein.
Im Garten draußen, unvermischt mit mir,
hätte sie bleiben müssen oder hingehn,—
nun währt sie so: was ist ihr mein Bewußtsein?

    Erschrick nicht, wenn ich jetzt begreife, ach,
da steigt es in mir auf: ich kann nicht anders,
ich muß begreifen, und wenn ich dran stürbe.
Begreifen, daß du hier bist. Ich begreife.
Ganz wie ein Blinder rings ein Ding begreift,
fühl ich dein Los und weiß ihm keinen Namen.
Laß uns zusammen klagen, daß dich einer
aus deinem Spiegel nahm. Kannst du noch weinen?
Du kannst nicht. Deiner Tränen Kraft und Andrang
hast du verwandelt in dein reifes Anschaun
und warst dabei, jeglichen Saft in dir
so umzusetzen in ein starkes Dasein,
das steigt und kreist, im Gleichgewicht und blindlings.

The kind of gravity that does not exist
In the beyond of peaceful images?
Why does your posture show me your misgiving?
What makes you lay your body's contours out
Like lines upon your palm, so that henceforth,
Seeing them, I must read your fate in them?

Come in the candlelight. I do not fear
To look upon the dead. For when they come,
They have the right to stand there for a moment
Before our eyes, the same as other things.

Come here; we will be still a little while.
Look at this rose upon my writing-desk:
Is not the light round it just as reluctant
As that round you? It should not be here either.
Out in the garden, unconfused with me,
It should have stayed or perished, but instead
It's here: what does it care about my consciousness?

Don't be afraid if now I grasp, for oh,
I feel it rise in me, I cannot help it,
I have to grasp, and though it meant my death,
To grasp that you are here. There, I have grasped it.
Just as a blind man grasps something around him,
I feel your plight and know no name for it.
Come let us mourn together that someone
Pulled you out of your mirror. Can you cry still?
You can't. The strength and pressure of your tears
Is changed now to a riper looking-on.
You were about to channel all your sap
Into the currents of a stronger being
That rises up and flows, balanced and blind —

Da riß ein Zufall dich, dein letzter Zufall
riß dich zurück aus deinem fernsten Fortschritt
in eine Welt zurück, wo Säfte *wollen*.
Riß dich nicht ganz; riß nur ein Stück zuerst,
doch als um dieses Stück von Tag zu Tag
die Wirklichkeit so zunahm, daß es schwer ward,
da brauchtest du dich ganz: da gingst du hin
und brachst in Brocken dich aus dem Gesetz
mühsam heraus, weil du dich brauchtest. Da
trugst du dich ab und grubst aus deines Herzens
nachtwarmem Erdreich die noch grünen Samen,
daraus dein Tod aufkeimen sollte: deiner,
dein eigner Tod zu deinem eignen Leben.
Und aßest sie, die Körner deines Todes,
wie alle andern, aßest seine Körner,
und hattest Nachgeschmack in dir von Süße,
die du nicht meintest, hattest süße Lippen,
du: die schon innen in den Sinnen süß war.

O laß uns klagen. Weißt du, wie dein Blut
aus einem Kreisen ohnegleichen zögernd
und ungern wiederkam, da du es abriefst?
Wie es verwirrt des Leibes kleinen Kreislauf
noch einmal aufnahm; wie es voller Mißtraun
und Staunen eintrat in den Mutterkuchen
und von dem weiten Rückweg plötzlich müd war.
Du triebst es an, du stießest es nach vorn,
du zerrtest es zur Feuerstelle, wie
man eine Herde Tiere zerrt zum Opfer;
und wolltest noch, es sollte dabei froh sein.
Und du erzwangst es schließlich: es war froh
und lief herbei und gab sich hin. Dir schien,

Had chance not pulled you back, ultimate chance
That pulled you from your farthermost advancement
Into a world again where the blood *wills*.
Not all at once; only a piece at first;
But as from day to day around this piece
The realness added on and made it heavy,
You needed all of you: and so you went
And broke yourself out of the law in pieces
Painstakingly, because you needed you.
Then you went down and dug out of your heart's
Nocturnal earth and warmth the still-green seeds
From which your death was meant to sprout: your own,
Your special death, the death of all your life,
And ate them then and there, your seeds of death,
Ate the death-seed like any other seed,
And had an aftertaste of sweetness in you,
All unintended, sweetness on your lips,
You: who were sweet already in your senses.

   Oh let us mourn. Do you know how your blood,
Caught up in a circulation like no other,
Reluctantly came back because you called it?
With what confusion it took up again
The body's smaller circulation, and
With what amazed distrust entered the womb,
Suddenly weary from the long way back.
You drove it on; you pushed it to the fore,
You dragged it toward the furnace, as one drags
A herd of victims to the sacrifice,
And asked it to be happy in the bargain.
And finally you compelled it: it came running
And gave itself up happily. You thought,

weil du gewohnt warst an die andern Maße,
es wäre nur für eine Weile; aber
nun warst du in der Zeit, und Zeit ist lang.
Und Zeit geht hin, und Zeit nimmt zu, und Zeit
ist wie ein Rückfall einer langen Krankheit.

Wie war dein Leben kurz, wenn du's vergleichst
mit jenen Stunden, da du saßest und
die vielen Kräfte deiner vielen Zukunft
schweigend herabbogst zu dem neuen Kindkeim,
der wieder Schicksal war. O wehe Arbeit.
O Arbeit über alle Kraft. Du tatest
sie Tag für Tag, du schlepptest dich zu ihr
und zogst den schönen Einschlag aus dem Webstuhl
und brauchtest alle deine Fäden anders.
Und endlich hattest du noch Mut zum Fest.

Denn da's getan war, wolltest du belohnt sein,
wie Kinder, wenn sie bittersüßen Tee
getrunken haben, der vielleicht gesund macht.
So lohntest du dich: denn von jedem andern
warst du zu weit, auch jetzt noch; keiner hätte
ausdenken können, welcher Lohn dir wohltut.
Du wußtest es. Du saßest auf im Kindbett,
und vor dir stand ein Spiegel, der dir alles
ganz wiedergab. Nun war das alles *Du*
und ganz *davor,* und drinnen war nur Täuschung,
die schöne Täuschung jeder Frau, die gern
Schmuck umnimmt und das Haar kämmt und verändert.

So starbst du, wie die Frauen früher starben,
altmodisch starbst du in dem warmen Hause
den Tod der Wöchnerinnen, welche wieder
sich schließen wollen und es nicht mehr können,

Being accustomed to the other measures,
That it was only for a while; except
Now you were back in time, and time is long.
And time goes on, and time adds up, and time
Is like the relapse of a chronic sickness.

How short your life was in comparison
With these long hours where you sat before
The many energies of your great future
And calmly bent them down to the new child-seed,
Which was a fate once more. Oh bitter labor,
Labor beyond all strength. And yet you did it.
Day after day you dragged yourself to work
And pulled the lovely weaving from the loom
And used your threads again a different way —
And finally put good face on your bad fortune.

When it was done, you wanted your reward
Like children when they've drunk bitter sweet tea
That hopefully will make them well again.
You found your own reward; you were too distant,
As always, from all others for another
To have imagined what reward would please you.
But you knew, and you sat up in your childbed.
And there before you was a looking-glass
That gave you back yourself completely. Now
That was all *you*, all *out there*, and inside
Only the sweet deceit of every woman
Who puts on jewels and combs and styles her hair.

And so you died, as women used to die,
Old-fashioned dying in a cozy house,
The death of women in their childbearing
Who try to close themselves again and can't

weil jenes Dunkel, das sie mitgebaren,
noch einmal wiederkommt und drängt und eintritt.
   Ob man nicht dennoch hätte Klagefrauen
auftreiben müssen? Weiber, welche weinen
für Geld, und die man so bezahlen kann,
daß sie die Nacht durch heulen, wenn es still wird.
Gebräuche her! wir haben nicht genug
Gebräuche. Alles geht und wird verredet.
So mußt du kommen, tot, und hier mit mir
Klagen nachholen. Hörst du, daß ich klage?
Ich möchte meine Stimme wie ein Tuch
hinwerfen über deines Todes Scherben
und zerrn an ihr, bis sie in Fetzen geht,
und alles, was ich sage, müßte so
zerlumpt in dieser Stimme gehn und frieren;
blieb es beim Klagen. Doch jetzt klag ich an:
den Einen nicht, der dich aus dir zurückzog,
(ich find ihn nicht heraus, er ist wie alle)
doch alle klag ich in ihm an: den Mann.
   Wenn irgendwo ein Kindgewesensein
tief in mir aufsteigt, das ich noch nicht kenne,
vielleicht das reinste Kindsein meiner Kindheit:
ich wills nicht wissen. Einen Engel will
ich daraus bilden ohne hinzusehn
und will ihn werfen in die erste Reihe
schreiender Engel, welche Gott erinnern.
   Denn dieses Leiden dauert schon zu lang,
und keiner kanns; es ist zu schwer für uns,
das wirre Leiden von der falschen Liebe,
die, bauend auf Verjährung wie Gewohnheit,
ein Recht sich nennt und wuchert aus dem Unrecht.

Because the darkness they also bore
Comes back again and forces its way in.

   But even so, shouldn't someone have hired
Some wailing-women? Women who weep for money,
And who, if you pay them right, will start a wail
At any hour of the night that grows too still.
More customs, please! We're running short on customs.
Everything goes and falls into disuse.
So you, the dead one, must come here to me
To get your mourning. Do you hear me mourn?
I wish my voice could be a cloth for you,
To drape across the fragments of your death;
I'd rip at it until it was in shreds,
And everything I say would have to go
Ragged and freezing in this voice — if just
Complaints were needed. But now I accuse:
Not the man who pulled you out of yourself
(I cannot find him out; he's like the others),
But I accuse them all in him: the Man.

   If there should rise from deep within me somewhere
A child-that-has-been, something yet unknown,
Perhaps the purest childhood of my childhood,
I do not want to know of it. I'll take it
And shape it into an angel without looking,
And I will throw it into the first row
Of screaming angels that remind the Lord.

   For all this suffering has gone on too long.
No one can keep it up; it is too hard for us,
The crazy suffering of an unjust love,
That, building on seniority and habit,
Claims rights and lets injustice grow like weeds.

Wo ist ein Mann, der Recht hat auf Besitz?
Wer kann besitzen, was sich selbst nicht hält,
was sich von Zeit zu Zeit nur selig auffängt
und wieder hinwirft wie ein Kind den Ball.
Sowenig wie der Feldherr eine Nike
festhalten kann am Vorderbug des Schiffes,
wenn das geheime Leichtsein ihrer Gottheit
sie plötzlich weghebt in den hellen Meerwind:
so wenig kann einer von uns die Frau
anrufen, die uns nicht mehr sieht und die
auf einem schmalen Streifen ihres Daseins
wie durch ein Wunder forgeht, ohne Unfall:
er hätte denn Beruf und Lust zur Schuld.
　　Denn *das* ist Schuld, wenn irgendeines Schuld ist:
die Freiheit eines Lieben nicht vermehren
um alle Freiheit, die man in sich aufbringt.
Wir haben, wo wir lieben, ja nur dies:
einander lassen; denn daß wir uns halten,
das fällt uns leicht und ist nicht erst zu lernen.

　　Bist du noch da? In welcher Ecke bist du? —
Du hast so viel gewußt von alledem
und hast so viel gekonnt, da du so hingingst
für alles offen, wie ein Tag, der anbricht.
Die Frauen leiden: lieben heißt allein sein,
und Künstler ahnen manchmal in der Arbeit,
daß sie verwandeln müssen, wo sie lieben.
Beides begannst du; beides ist in Dem,
was jetzt ein Ruhm entstellt, der es dir fortnimmt.
Ach du warst weit von jedem Ruhm. Du warst
unscheinbar; hattest leise deine Schönheit

Where is the man who has the right to own?
And who can own what does not keep itself
But only sometimes makes a happy catch
And throws it back again like a child's ball.
As little as the captain can hold fast
To winged Victory figured on his bow
When, by the secret lightness of her godhead,
She is whisked off into the sparkling sea-wind:
So little can we call out to the woman
Who does not see us any more but walks
Miraculously, without accident,
On down the narrow strip of her existence —
Unless we have a taste for what is wrong.

For that is wrong, if anything is wrong:
Not to increase the freedom of a loved one
By all the freedom that you find in you.
And everywhere we love, we have but this:
To let each other go; since holding on
Is easy, and we don't have to learn it first.

Are you still there? What corner are you in?
You used to know so much of everything,
Could do so many things, as you walked out
Open to everything like breaking day.
Women suffer, true lovers are alone,
And artists at their labors sometimes sense
That everywhere they love, they must work change.
You started to do both; both are in that
Which fame distorts in taking it away.
But you were distant from all fame. You were
Inconspicuous, having softly taken

hineingenommen, wie man eine Fahne
einzieht am grauen Morgen eines Werktags,
und wolltest nichts, als eine lange Arbeit,—
die nicht getan ist: dennoch nicht getan.
    Wenn du noch da bist, wenn in diesem Dunkel
noch eine Stelle ist, an der dein Geist
empfindlich mitschwingt auf den flachen Schallwelln,
die eine Stimme, einsam in der Nacht,
aufregt in eines hohen Zimmers Strömung:
So hör mich: Hilf mir. Sieh, wir gleiten so,
nicht wissend wann, zurück aus unserm Fortschritt
in irgendwas, was wir nicht meinen; drin
wir uns verfangen wie in einem Traum
und drin wir sterben, ohne zu erwachen.
Keiner ist weiter. Jedem, der sein Blut
hinaufhob in ein Werk, das lange wird,
kann es geschehen, daß ers nicht mehr hochhält
und daß es geht nach seiner Schwere, wertlos.
Denn irgendwo ist eine alte Feindschaft
zwischen dem Leben und der großen Arbeit.
Daß ich sie einseh und sie sage: hilf mir.
    Komm nicht zurück. Wenn du's erträgst, so sei
tot bei den Toten. Tote sind beschäftigt.
Doch hilf mir so, daß es dich nicht zerstreut,
wie mir das Fernste manchmal hilft: in mir.

Your beauty in, as one takes down a pennant
On the gray morning of a working day.
You wanted nothing but a lifetime's work,
Which is undone for all that, still undone.
  If you are still there, if within this darkness
There still is any spot in which your spirit
Vibrates in sympathy with the shallow soundwaves
Which, lonely in the night, a single voice
Stirs up in the currents of a high-walled room,
Then hear me: help me. See; we are afloat,
Not knowing when we'll slide out of our progress
And into something we don't mean, in which
We get ourselves caught up as in a dream
And die in it and never do wake up:
No one is wiser. Anyone who puts
His blood into a lifelong work can find
One day he just can't keep holding it up there
And so its worthless poundage drags it down:
Because there is an ancient enmity,
Somewhere, between man's life and his great works.
That I may see it and may say it, help me.
Come back no more. If you can bear it, be
Dead with the dead. The dead are occupied.
Help me so that it does not scatter you,
As things most distant often help: in me.

LYRIC POEMS

KLAGE

O wie ist alles fern
und lange vergangen.
Ich glaube, der Stern,
von welchem ich Glanz empfange,
ist seit Jahrtausenden tot.
Ich glaube, im Boot,
das vorüberfuhr,
hörte ich etwas Banges sagen.
Im Hause hat eine Uhr
geschlagen . . .
In welchem Haus? . . .
Ich möchte aus meinem Herzen hinaus
unter den großen Himmel treten.
Ich möchte beten.
Und einer von allen Sternen
müßte wirklich noch sein.
Ich glaube, ich wüßte,
welcher allein
gedauert hat,—
welcher wie eine weiße Stadt
am Ende des Strahls in den Himmeln steht . . .

LAMENT

How everything is far
and lost and gone.
I think the star
whose brightness I welcome in
has been extinct for an age.
I think, in the barge
that passed, a voice was afraid.
Back in the house a clock
went dead . . .
But in what house? . . .
If I could only get out
of my heart and under the wide sky.
If I could pray.
Surely of all the stars, one
must still be there.
I think I'd know
which one alone
has lasted through; which one
at the beam's end in heaven stands like a silver town.

PONT DU CARROUSEL

Der blinde Mann, der auf der Brücke steht,
grau wie ein Markstein namenloser Reiche,
er ist vielleicht das Ding, das immer gleiche,
um das von fern die Sternenstunde geht,
und der Gestirne stiller Mittelpunkt.
Denn alles um ihn irrt und rinnt und prunkt.

Er ist der unbewegliche Gerechte,
in viele wirre Wege hingestellt;
der dunkle Eingang in die Unterwelt
bei einem oberflächlichen Geschlechte.

PONT DU CARROUSEL

The sightless man upon the bridge who stands,
Gray like the boundarystone of nameless ranges,
He is perhaps the thing, that never changes,
Round which the mainspring of the heavens winds,
The distant planets' center of repose;
For all around him runs and bumps and goes.

He is the upright sentry at his station,
Set down in many paths perplexed and whorled,
The darkling entry to the underworld
Amidst a surface-loving generation.

ABEND

Der Abend wechselt langsam die Gewänder,
die ihm ein Rand von alten Bäumen hält;
du schaust: und von dir scheiden sich die Länder,
ein himmelfahrendes und eins, das fällt;

und lassen dich, zu keinem ganz gehörend,
nicht ganz so dunkel wie das Haus, das schweigt,
nicht ganz so sicher Ewiges beschwörend
wie das, was Stern wird jede Nacht und steigt —

und lassen dir (unsäglich zu entwirrn)
dein Leben bang und riesenhaft und reifend,
so daß es, bald begrenzt und bald begreifend,
abwechselnd Stein in dir wird und Gestirn.

EVENING

The evening pauses for a change of vesture,
Which trees hold ready in their patient hands;
You watch, and see the lands in their departure,
A land ascending, and a falling land;

Which leave you there, in neither land quite resting,
Less darksome than the house benumbed in time,
Less able to conjure the everlasting
Than that which turns to star each night and climbs —

And leave to you, entangled and bizarre,
Your life, foreboding and immense and rising,
A thing that, now confined and now comprising,
Reverberates as stone in you and star.

Aus "LIEDER DER MÄDCHEN"

Die Zeit, von der die Mütter sprachen,
fand nicht zu unsern Schlafgemachen,
und drin blieb alles glatt und klar.
Sie sagen uns, daß sie zerbrachen
in einem sturmgejagten Jahr.

Wir wissen nicht: Was ist das, Sturm?

Wir wohnen immer tief im Turm
und hören manchmal nur von fern
die Wälder draußen wehn;
und einmal blieb ein fremder Stern
bei uns stehn.

Und wenn wir dann im Garten sind,
so zittern wir, daß es beginnt,
und warten Tag um Tag —

aber nirgends ist ein Wind,
der uns biegen mag.

FROM "LIEDER DER MÄDCHEN"

Young girls sing:
The time of which our mothers told,
It never reached inside the fold
Where we lay sleeping, smooth and clear.
They say to us that they were felled
By thunderstorms, one stormy year.

What is a storm? We cannot say.

Deep in our tower tucked away
We have to listen from afar
To hear the forest sigh.
One night there was a strange star
That passed by.

And in the garden where we sing,
We tremble, feeling it begin;
Each day we are on guard -

But nowhere is there any wind
To bend us hard.

LIEBES-LIED

Wie soll ich meine Seele halten, daß
sie nicht an deine rührt? Wie soll ich sie
hinheben über dich zu andern Dingen?
Ach gerne möcht ich sie bei irgendwas
Verlorenem im Dunkel unterbringen
an einer fremden stillen Stelle, die
nicht weiterschwingt, wenn deine Tiefen schwingen.
Doch alles, was uns anrührt, dich und mich,
nimmt uns zusammen wie ein Bogenstrich,
der aus zwei Saiten *eine* Stimme zieht.
Auf welches Instrument sind wir gespannt?
Und welcher Geiger hat uns in der Hand?
O süßes Lied.

LOVESONG

How should I keep my soul in bounds, that it
May not graze against yours? How should I raise
It over you to other things above it?
Ah, if I only knew of someplace lost
That lies in darkness, I would gladly leave it
There in a strange and silent place, somewhere
Where all your depths may swing, and will not move it.
But all the things that touch us, me and you,
Take us together like a stroking bow
As from two strings it draws one voice along.
Upon what instrument have we been spanned?
And who the fiddler has us in his hand?
O sweet the song.

EINSAMKEIT

Die Einsamkeit ist wie ein Regen.
Sie steigt vom Meer den Abenden entgegen;
von Ebenen, die fern sind und entlegen,
geht sie zum Himmel, der sie immer hat.
Und erst vom Himmel fällt sie auf die Stadt.

Regnet hernieder in den Zwitterstunden,
wenn sich nach Morgen wenden alle Gassen
und wenn die Leiber, welche nichts gefunden,
enttäuscht und traurig von einander lassen;
und wenn die Menschen, die einander hassen,
in *einem* Bett zusammen schlafen müssen:

dann geht die Einsamkeit mit den Flüssen ...

THE LONELINESS

The loneliness is like a rain.
It rises toward the evening from the main.
Up from the surfaces of distant plains
It gains the sky, its home. And only down
From out the sky it falls upon the town.

It drizzles downward in the halfway watches
When all the alleys turn and head for morning;
And when, no wiser for their one-night matches,
The bodies part, and set about returning;
And when the ones with hatred in them burning
Must share their bed, and cannot share their dreams;

Then loneliness down rivers and streams . . .

DIE FLAMINGOS
Paris, Jardin des Plantes

In Spiegelbildern wie von Fragonard
ist doch von ihrem Weiß und ihrer Röte
nicht mehr gegeben, als dir einer böte,
wenn er von seiner Freundin sagt: sie war

noch sanft von Schlaf. Denn steigen sie ins Grüne
und stehn, auf rosa Stielen leicht gedreht,
beisammen, blühend, wie in einem Beet,
verführen sie, verführender als Phryne

sich selber; bis sie ihres Auges Bleiche
hinhalsend bergen in der eignen Weiche,
in welcher Schwarz und Fruchtrot sich versteckt.

Auf einmal kreischt ein Neid durch die Voliere;
sie aber haben sich erstaunt gestreckt
und schreiten einzeln ins Imaginäre.

THE FLAMINGOS

In mirror images like Fragonard's
Is nothing of their redness nor their whiteness
Beyond what could be given in a likeness,
Saying about a lovely girl: *She was*

Still soft with sleep. For if, amid the planting,
On coral stems adroitly pivoted,
They stand in clumps, like blossoms in a bed,
They court themselves with courtship more enchanting

Than Phryne's: till their necks reflex to harbor
Their pale eyes in their own sweet feather-arbor,
Where black and apple-red in hiding lies.

A sudden envy shrieks through the partition;
They, having stretched themselves in arch surprise,
Go stalking off into sheer supposition.

DIE GAZELLE
Gazella Dorcas

Verzauberte: wie kann der Einklang zweier
erwählter Worte je den Reim erreichen,
der in dir kommt und geht, wie auf ein Zeichen.
Aus deiner Stirne steigen Laub und Leier,

und alles Deine geht schon im Vergleich
durch Liebeslieder, deren Worte, weich
wie Rosenblätter, dem, der nicht mehr liest,
sich auf die Augen legen, die er schließt:

um dich zu sehen: hingetragen, als
wäre mit Sprüngen jeder Lauf geladen
und schösse nur nicht ab, solang der Hals

das Haupt ins Horchen hält: wie wenn beim Baden
im Wald die Badende sich unterbricht:
den Waldsee im gewendeten Gesicht.

THE GAZELLE

Enchanted creature, how can words aspire,
Though paired in tune, to learn the rhyming spells
That come and go in you like signal-bells?
From out your forehead rises leaf and lyre;

A likeness sends your qualities aloft
In songs of love, in which the lyrics, soft
As roseleaves, settle on the hand that puts
A volume down, and on the eye that shuts

To look at you: transported, so to speak
As if the legs were charged with ammunition,
Kept back for now from springing while the neck
Holds up the head to hear — in such a fashion
As when the woodland bather halts in place,
The forest lake in her averted face.

DER PANTHER
Im Jardin des Plantes, Paris

Sein Blick ist vom Vorübergehn der Stäbe
so müd geworden, daß er nichts mehr hält.
Ihm ist, als ob es tausend Stäbe gäbe
und hinter tausend Stäben keine Welt.

Der weiche Gang geschmeidig starker Schritte,
der sich im allerkleinsten Kreise dreht,
ist wie ein Tanz von Kraft um eine Mitte,
in der betäubt ein großer Wille steht.

Nur manchmal schiebt der Vorhang der Pupille
sich lautlos auf —. Dann geht ein Bild hinein,
geht durch der Glieder angespannte Stille —
und hört im Herzen auf zu sein.

THE PANTHER

His gaze, from the revolving bars that bound him,
Has grown so weary that it will not hold,
As if there were a thousand bars around him,
And then behind the thousand bars no world.

The supple steps, here hardened and here softened,
Turned round upon each other like a spring,
Suggest a dance of strength around a deafened
Will, fixed in the center of the ring.

At random points of time the pupil's valance
Goes softly up: A picture hits the eyes,
Goes through the members in their tightened silence,
And reaches to the heart and dies.

DAS ABENDMAHL

Sie sind versammelt, staunende Verstörte,
um ihn, der wie ein Weiser sich beschließt
und der sich fortnimmt denen er gehörte
und der an ihnen fremd vorüberfließt.
Die alte Einsamkeit kommt über ihn,
die ihn erzog zu seinem tiefen Handeln;
nun wird er wieder durch den Ölwald wandeln,
und die ihn lieben werden vor ihm fliehn.

Er hat sie zu dem letzten Tisch entboten
und (wie ein Schuß die Vögel aus den Schoten
scheucht) scheucht er ihre Hände aus den Broten
mit seinem Wort: sie fliegen zu ihm her;
sie flattern bange durch die Tafelrunde
und suchen einen Ausgang. Aber *er*
ist überall wie eine Dämmerstunde.

THE LAST SUPPER

They sit assembled, credulous and furtive,
With him who like a sage is closed in thought,
Who takes himself from these whom he was part of,
And flows beyond their heads, and knows them not.
He feels the coming-on of loneliness,
In which his deep necessity was nourished;
Now he will wander in the olive forest;
Who love him most, will flee him in distress.

He asked to eat with them before he leaves;
And, as a bullet scatters birds from sheaves
Of grain, he scatters their fingers from the loaves
With this, his word. They crumple at his knee;
They flutter vaguely through the hall, intending
To find a window or a door. But he
Is all around them, like the dusk descending.

HERBSTTAG

Herr: es ist Zeit. Der Sommer war sehr groß.
Leg deinen Schatten auf die Sonnenuhren,
und auf den Fluren laß die Winde los.

Befiehl den letzten Früchten voll zu sein;
gib ihnen noch zwei südlichere Tage,
dränge sie zur Vollendung hin und jage
die letzte Süße in den schweren Wein.

Wer jetzt kein Haus hat, baut sich keines mehr.
Wer jetzt allein ist, wird es lange bleiben,
wird wachen, lesen, lange Briefe schreiben
und wird in den Alleen hin und her
unruhig wandern, wenn die Blätter treiben.

AUTUMN DAY

Lord: it is time. The summer has been large.
Lay down across the sundialface thy shadow,
And on the meadow set the winds at large.

Command the fruit be heavy on the vine;
Give them two southern-winded days of leisure;
Propel them to complete themselves; and pressure
The final sweetness in the heavy wine.

Whoever has no house now, goes without.
Whoever lacks a friend, will long be lacking,
Will spend his time in writing, reading, waking,
And through the tree-lined avenues in and out

Restlessly wandering, when the leaves are flaking.